Bria                                                    ; wife
Ann                                                  e. He
spen                                                r half
perf                                              . He
rema                                             and
crow                                           n-day
desc

Pete                                            long
as h                                          ound
100                                          and
Steg                                          been
draw                                         illion
year                                         doing
this                                        T-Rex
has

Other books in the **TIME FOR A RHYME** series:

## MAGNIFICENT MACHINES
poems chosen by John Foster

## SPECTACULAR SPOOKS
poems chosen by Brian Moses

## FREAKY FAMILIES
poems chosen by David Orme

## WACKY WILD ANIMALS
poems chosen by Brian Moses

## PECULIAR PETS
poems chosen by Brian Moses

# DANGEROUS DINOSAURS

## Chosen by Brian Moses

### Illustrated by Peter Allen

MACMILLAN CHILDREN'S BOOKS

First published 2002
by Macmillan Children's Books
a division of Macmillan Publishers Limited
20 New Wharf Road, London N1 9RR
Basingstoke and Oxford
www.panmacmillan.com

Associated companies throughout the world

ISBN 0 330 39152 6

35798642

A CIP catalogue record for this book is available from the British Library.

Printed by Mackays of Chatham plc, Chatham, Kent.

'Neversaurus' by Celia Warren first published in *Penny Whistle Pete* by Collins Educational 1995

# Contents

# I Wish I Was a Dinosaur

I wish I was a dinosaur
with flashing eyes and monster roar.
I wish I had great stomping feet
and other dinosaurs to eat.
I'd gallop down the jungle trail
with gnashing teeth and lashing tail.
Those other dinosaurs would run
and me? I would be having fun
as really, I am rather small
and don't scare anyone at all.

*Marian Swinger*

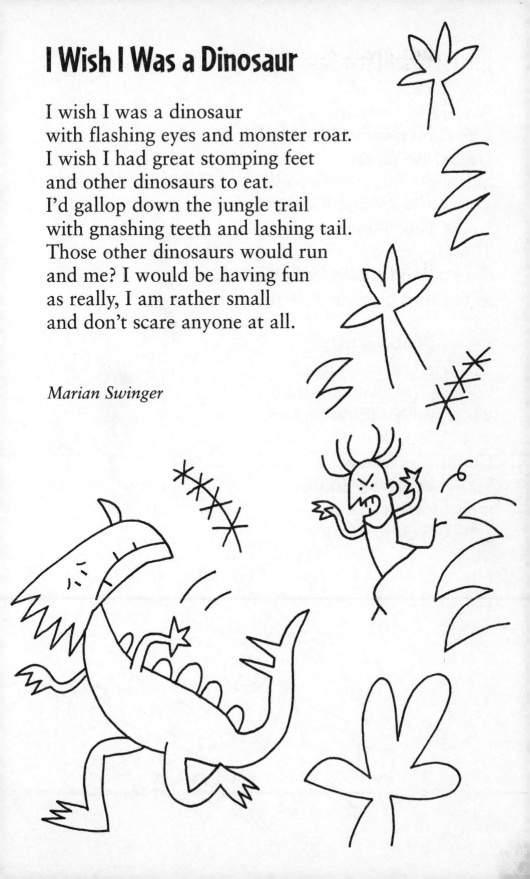

# Jurassic Lark

Act like a dinosaur
when you go to school.
Go on! Be Jurassic,
kids will think you're cool.

Stomp like a Sesimosaurus!
Thunder, rumble, shake,
thump, bump, bang, crash, wallop.
Make your classroom shake.

Scavenge like a T-Rex!
Tear, rip, gobble, crunch,
burp, belch, dribble, slobber,
when you eat school lunch.

Go on! Act Jurassic!
See what teacher thinks.
If she doesn't like it
act like you're extinct!

*Jane Clarke*

# Raptor Rap

I'm a speedy hunter,
I'm a carnivore
I like my meat
And I like it RAW!
Can you feel my breath?
Can you see my claws?
You'll be scared to death
When I clash my jaws.
I'll slice you up
Into little pieces
I'll share your bones
With my nephews and nieces.
You can be my captive,
And I'll be your captor,
If you'll rap with me –
I'm Velociraptor.

*Clare Bevan*

# Did Dinosaurs Go to the Dentist?

Did dinosaurs go to the dentist?
Did they go for a filling or two?
Did they sit in the chair and look up
Just like you and me do?

Did they open their mouths really wide
To show off their bright red gums?
And did the dentist give them all stickers
If he didn't end up in their tums?!

*Coral Rumble*

# Dinah

Dinah thumps and trundles,
Dinah stamps and shakes,
Dinah speaks like thunder,
Dinah makes earthquakes,
Dinah scares the children,
Dinah rocks and roars,
Dinah leaps from the mountains
Then guess what . . .
Dinah soars!

*Daphne Kitching*

# Down at the Dinosaur Fair

You can turn,
you can twist
in the prehistoric mist,
feel the dampness in your hair.
You can sprint,
you can spin
from a big bony chin
        down at the Dinosaur Fair!

You can swoop,
you can swing
from a dark leather wing
and fly through pillows of air.
You can slip,
you can slide
on a scaly scarlet hide
        down at the Dinosaur Fair!

You can zing,
you can zoom
down a backbone flume,
whiz round in a waltzing chair.
You can whip,
you can whack
on a slippery saddle back
        down at the Dinosaur Fair!

You can trip
you can trek
up a narrow bendy neck
any day, any time, anywhere.
You can flail,
you can float
like a wave-tossed boat
　　　down at the Dinosaur Fair!


*John Rice*

# Dinosauristory

Hocus, pocus,
plodding through the swamp;
I'm a Diplodocus,
*chomp, chomp, chomp!*

Grass for breakfast,
I could eat a tree!
Grass for lunch and dinner
and grass for tea.

I'm a Diplodocus
plodding through the swamp,
hocus, rocus, pocus,
*chomp, chomp, chomp!*

*Judith Nicholls*

# Dinosaur in the Garden

Believe me if you dare
Or believe me *not,* I don't care
But late last night
There was a dinosaur in my garden.

Oh yes there was!

I could hear it stomping across the ground
Then throwing the dustbins all around
And ripping branches from the trees
Then pulling tiles off our roof with ease.

Oh yes there was!

So believe me if you dare
Or believe me *not,* I don't care
But when I woke up early this morning
I could still hear it rumbling in the distance.

*Ian Souter*

# Shudder

Some dinosaurs
were so HUGE and HEAVY
that when I think of them
TRAMPING and TRAMPING
the Earth

even though they've been gone
for many millions of years

I feel their VIBRATIONS

and SHUDDER.

*Philip Waddell*

# My Christmas Present

I asked for a dinosaur for Christmas,
and there it was all shining and new.
But it grew ever so quickly
then flapped its wings and away it flew.
Next year I want one that doesn't fly!

*Janis Priestley*

# Duvetsaurus Featherfill

The world at night belongs to me
As I close my bedroom door.
I lie awake and wait for him,
My secret dinosaur!
Duvetsaurus Featherfill
Who no one else has found,
I met him first one sleepless night
As he was prowling round
And round my bunk bed
Feeling restless, just like me.
As I tossed and wriggled
Duvetsaurus copied me.

We have some great adventures,
He changes shape each night,
From long and flat while sleeping
To tall and fat, to fight.
Not only can his shape change,
But his pattern can as well.
Every week, on washday,
(Just as he begins to smell)
He cleverly transforms himself
To blend in with my bed,
So no one ever knows he's there
But him and me . . . and Ted.

*Daphne Kitching*

# The Grumposaurus

Each morning a grumposaurus
tears into our bedroom,
she burrows down
beneath the duvet
and roars out commands
most grumposaurusly:
"Where's my drink?"
"I want a story!"

We really have to take care
not to annoy this beast,
give her milk and cereal,
a TV cartoon or two.
Then at times the grumposaurus
can be quite friendly,
she hugs and smothers us,
tries to mother us . . .

But we never know when
she'll turn grumposaurus,
we never know when,
mouth wide, she'll roar at us,
or sit in a huff
and just ignore us.
It's a tough life
living with a grumposaurus.

*Brian Moses*

# Neversaurus

When dinosaurs roamed the earth,
So huge it was easy to spot 'em,
You'd frequently see a triceratops,
But never a tricerabottom.

*Celia Warren*

# Dinosaur Adventure Playground

It's great to slide down the neck of a Brontosaurus,
Swing to and fro on the legs of a Pterodactyl,
Use the Stegosaurus as a climbing frame
But no way is the Triceratops a bouncy castle.

*Paul Cookson*

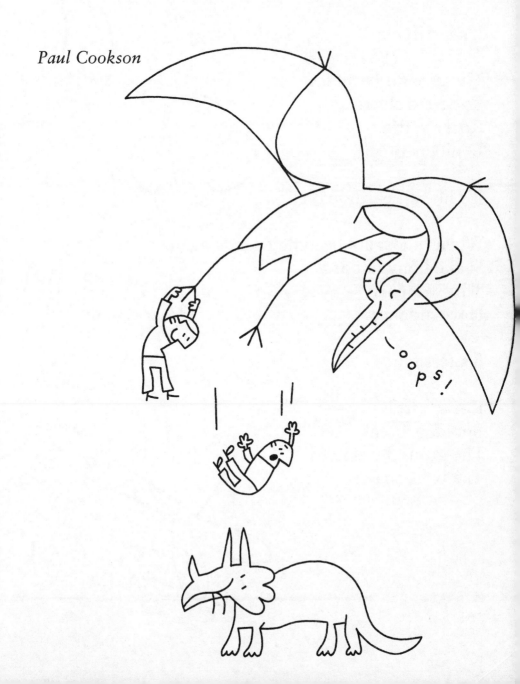

# Quake

When dinosaurs have a falling out
When dinosaurs have a fight
Anyone with any sense
Keeps well out of sight

It's terrifying!

The ground trembles
The trees shake
Rocks rattle
Boulders break

It's like an earthquake!

When dinosaurs become friends again
Shake bony hands
Throw a party
Have a dance

It's terrifying!

Rocks rattle
Boulders break
The ground trembles
The trees shake

BASH!

snap!

But those with sense don't go shouting:
"Be quiet, for goodness sake!"
They lie low
and quake.

Bernard Young

# I Thought I Saw

I thought I saw
A dinosaur
Grazing in the park.

I saw it, I thought,
In the evening mist
When all was growing dark.

It began to lumber towards me.
I turned at once and fled.
For, I confess, I was terrified
Of this creature long since dead.

I ran and ran on weary legs,
Afraid that I might die.
Behind I could sense
Its hot, hot breath.
The sun seemed to slip
From the sky.

At last, I reached my home sweet home.
I rushed in and slammed the door.
My mother asked why I looked so pale
And what I was panting for.

When I told her she just laughed and laughed.
She said: "Dinosaurs don't exist."

But she doesn't know
What I saw and I felt
Out there in the dark park mist!

*John Kitching*

# I Saw a Little Brontosaurus

I saw a little Brontosaurus
    dancing in the sink.
"Hello," I said, "you lizard thing –
    you ought to be extinct!

"Why are you dancing to the tunes
    on our kitchen radio
when all your mates died out, they say,
    millions of years ago?

"And then your size. You're meant to be
    as long as our High Street
with fat tum and big bottom
    and fearsome thumping feet?"

The little bronto stared at me.
    He nibbled the kettle flex.
He waddled away from my best pet
    Tyrannosaurus Rex.

*Fred Sedgwick*

# Tyrannosaurus Rex

With old cardboard boxes
And polystyrene,
It looks the best
There's ever been.

Torches for eyes
Knives for teeth,
No one can guess
What's underneath.

When I'm inside
It's really fun,
To go round
Scaring everyone.


*Ian Larmont*

grrr

# Terrorsaur

Run little dinosaur, run, run, run.
There's a shadow from something BIG
blocking out the sun.

Not from a tree, not from a cloud.
It's the shadow of something
fierce and LOUD.

With its spiky teeth and growling ROAR
it's a hungry, hunting *terror*-saur.


*Penny Kent*

# Flymo Dino

Now many of the dinosaurs
Ate only plants and leaves,
Nibbling long and lovingly
As peaceful as you please.

And that's why grass was always short
Around a munching dino,
He was, you see, a grass cutter –
A prehistoric Flymo.

*Clive Webster*

# Why Our Teacher Knows Everything about Dinosaurs

Mister Whitmore says dinosaurs lived
a long, long, long, long, long, long time ago.
Hundreds and hundreds and hundreds
and thousands and thousands and thousands
and millions and millions and millions
of years ago.

I believe him.
He should know.
He was there.

*Paul Cookson*

The Whitmorosaure

# Why the Dinosaur Became Extinct

The reason for the extinction
Of the whole of the dinosaur race
Is that one day the Earth began spinning so fast
They were all flung off into space.

*John Foster*

# Dinosaurs Aren't Dead

Dinosaurs aren't dead
it's all been a mistake
they're still alive,
they're all wide awake.

For dinosaurs are back
they really are here,
it would take more than a meteorite
to make them disappear.

They rifle round dustbins
in the middle of the night,
you'll know one is near
when cats freeze with fright.

They live under bridges
from railways now still,
but appear in the shadows
when the moon starts to fill.

They rush round each night
in a special disguise,
you might spot those tails
and staring deep eyes.

They leave giant footprints
wherever they've been,
and, if you look twice,
they can sometimes be seen.

So if you ever awake
to a terrible roar,
it will just be the sound
of an old dinosaur!

*Andrew Collett*

# The Binbagosaurus

With one great glassy eye at the front
And a huge, gaping jaw at the back,
The Binbagosaurus crawls down our street:
Won't you feed it a black plastic sack?

Rushing round, fearful humans all fling
Bulging sack after sack in its jaw,
And it grinds and it smashes and minces and
    mashes,
Then it burps, "Feed me more, feed me more!"

Every house in the street must supply it
With one bag – some houses send more.
If you fail to deliver, it might eat your fence
Or your gate – or perhaps your front door.

O, beware the Binbagosaurus –
Its mind may change all of a sudden:
It could just get tired of eating black bags –
Then it might fancy you for its pudding!

*Eric Finney*

# The Dinosaur Stomp

They were doing the dinosaur stomp,
dinosaurs out for a romp,
dinosaurs tramping
stomping and stamping,
dancing their way round the swamp.

The earth shook, the tall tree ferns swayed
with the terrible noise that they made
with their clattering claws
and their ear-splitting roars
as they joined in the stomping parade.

Pterodactyls swooped round them like kites
as the moon splashed their figures with white
and their eyes glowed and shone
as the stomping went on
and shattered the peace of the night.

In the morning, they lay in a heap,
worn out and all fast asleep.
There was peace for a while
as they snored in a pile,
two or three dinosaurs deep.

*Marian Swinger*

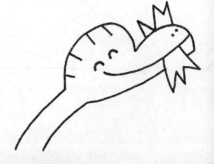

# Pity Poor Diplodocus

Pity poor Diplodocus –
great lumbering mass of meat.
It took so long for messages
to go from brain to feet.
He'd wander straight into a bog,
or off a cliff,
or worse,
before a message from his brain
could make his feet reverse.

*Barry Buckingham*

# Jurassic United F.C.

The wingers are two Pterodactyls,
Two Velociraptors make up the attack;
A mega-Stegasaurus is the goalie,
Two Triceratops are at full-back.

Three T-Rexes in the mid-field
Are absolute dynamite;
The sweeper's a Diplodocus
Who likes to keep things tight!

The best ever in History.
The best there's ever been;
JURASSIC UNITED F.C. –
Massive, magnificent and mean!

*Tony Langham*

# It's Obvious Really

The mystery's been solved at last –
Why many a dinosaur
Had great long necks ten metres long
Way, way above the floor.

The reason is, we've just found out –
And it really makes you chortle –
The dinosaurs had great long necks
Because their feet smelled awful!

*Clive Webster*

# In Praise of Dinosaurs

For massive size and mighty strength
And all the bones along their length,
Dinosaurs
Deserve applause.

For having long and weird names
And ruling Earth despite small brains,
Dinosaurs
Deserve applause.

For spines and horns and huge footprints
And leaving lots of evidence,
Dinosaurs
Deserve applause.


*Emma Shaw*

# What Dino Saw

I know just what Dino saw –
He saw T-Rex's toothy jaw
And strong sharp claws
Which made him roar;

But he never saw
A revolving door,
Or visited a video store
Or waltzed across a ballroom floor –

But that's because
Poor Dino Saur
Was born too many years before!

*Dave Ward*

# A Tyrannosaur in Tesco's!

A Tyrannosaur in Tesco's
Came stomping down the aisle
Searching for the dental floss
And practising his smile.

Did the stegosaur in Sainsbury's
Want a trolley or a basket?
No one knew, and no one really
Had the nerve to ask it.

In W. H. Smith's I saw
A young velociraptor
Reading Enid Blyton
And devouring every chapter.

The camera girl in Boots
Was busy with a diplodocus
Demonstrating lenses
And explaining how to focus.

A megalosaur in M&S
Was tying something frilly
But checking in the mirror
Just to see if she looked silly.

The dinosaurs, all loaded down
With boxes, bags and bits
Then jumped into a taxi
To take coffee at The Ritz.

*Paul Bright*

# The Prehistoric Party

When Alice Allosaurus had a party
Pat Apatosaurus couldn't come.
Don Iguanadon was not invited,
So he sulked and sucked his thumb.

Tracey-Anne Triceratops was early.
Vanessa Plesiosaurus came in late
And pinched all the fairysaurus fingers
Off Terry Pterodactyl's plate.

Stella Stegosaurus won the first game,
Brian Brontosaurus won the next,
Then Ricky Rhamphorynchus caused a rumpus
When he beat Tyrannosaurus Rex.

So if you plan a prehistoric party,
Invite your friends to come in fancy dress,
Have jelly, cake, balloons and Pass the Parcel,
But don't ask Tyrannosaurus Rex.

*Celia Warren*

# If Dinosaurs Were Alive Today

If we still had dinosaurs,
if they hadn't died away,
what would we do with those
still alive today?

Would they all be put to work
cleaning windows right up high?
Would a dinosaur have the job
of directing planes across the sky?

Would they all be bodyguards
for pop stars or the Queen?
Would they be demolition workers
instead of some machine?

Would they all be road builders
trampling tarmac into place?
Would they all launch satellites
high up into space?

So if we still had dinosaurs
if they hadn't been swept away,
just what would we do with them
if they were alive today?

*Andrew Collett*

# Dinosaur Day

What sight do you see when you look at his neck?
    Did Dinah sword-dance on dinosaur day?
A rubbery tube of brown and black speck.
    Yes, Dinah sword-danced on dinosaur day.

What view do you get when you look at his head?
    Did Dinah sword-dance on dinosaur day?
A sharp cutting gap and two deep wells of red.
    Yes, Dinah sword-danced on dinosaur day.

What can your eyes tell when you look at his tail?
    Did Dinah sword-dance on dinosaur day?
An engine of force to help him set sail.
    Yes, Dinah sword-danced on dinosaur day.

What shape can you spy when you stare at his leg?
    Did Dinah sword-dance on dinosaur day?
A 'Z' and an 'S' both as smooth as an egg.
    Yes, Dinah sword-danced on dinosaur day.

Spy neck, spy speck, see head, see red.
    Sight tail, sight sail, spot egg, spot leg.
The beasts of the sea sang the words of the bay
    When Dinah sword-danced on dinosaur day.

*John Rice*

# Baby Dinosaur

I found a baby dinosaur
asleep in the garden shed.
So I carried it ever so carefully
and tucked it up in my bed.

My mum and dad don't know it yet.
I think they're in for a fright.
That sweet little baby dinosaur
has grown quite big in the night.


*Tony Mitton*

# Dinosaur Diets

If a brontosaurus
ever stood before us,
it would simply explore us
and then – ignore us;
for in the stomach of a brontosaurus,
plants always came before us!

But if a tyrannosaurus
came across us,
ever saw us,
it would simply adore us;
for in the stomach of a tyrannosaurus
is where they liked to **store us!**

*Ian Souter*

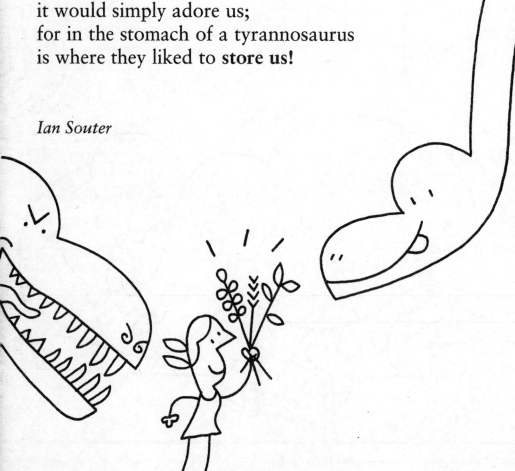